TOOL KIT

TAKE IT APART

Patty Whitehouse

Rourke
Publishing LLC
Vero Beach, Florida 32964

www.rourkepublishing.com

PHOTO CREDITS: © Lynn Stone: pages 4, 9, 11, 14, 15; © Armentrout: pages 5, 6, 7, 8, 10, 12, 13, 16, 17, 18, 22; © John Weise: page 19; © PIR: pages10, 12, 13, 16; © Craig Lopetz: page 20; © RJ Equipment Sales & Imports, Clearwater, FL: page 21

Editor: Robert Stengard-Olliges

Cover design by Nicola Stratford

Library of Congress Cataloging-in-Publication Data

Whitehouse, Patty, 1958-
  Take it apart : took kit / Patty Whitehouse.
     p. cm.
  Includes index.
  ISBN 1-60044-212-9 (hardcover)
  ISBN 1-59515-560-0 (softcover)
  1. Tools--Juvenile literature. I. Title.
  TJ1195.W52 2006
  621.9--dc22
                              2006010671

Printed in the USA

CG/CG

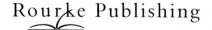

www.rourkepublishing.com – sales@rourkepublishing.com
Post Office Box 3328, Vero Beach, FL 32964

Table of Contents

How Do Tools Help People?

Tools are things that help do work. Tools have many shapes and sizes.

Some things are too big. Workers use tools to make them smaller.

Taking Things Apart

Tools help with many kinds of work. Some tools are for building. Some are for growing things.

The tools in this book help people take things apart.

Scissors and Tin Snips

Scissors have two sharp **edges**. They can cut paper.
They can cut cloth.

Tin snips look like big scissors. Tin snips cut things made of **metal**.

Wire Cutters

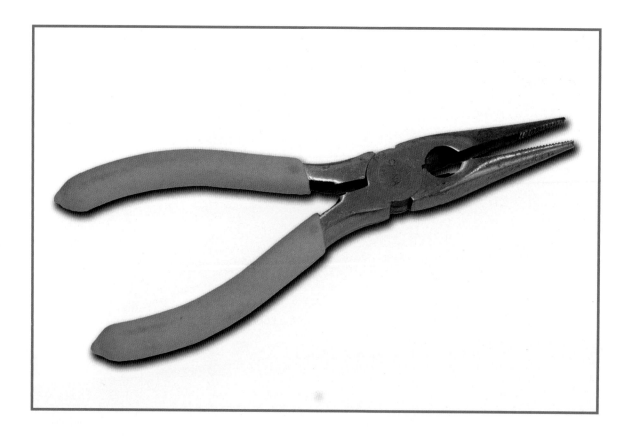

This is a wire cutter. **Electricians** use it to cut metal wires.

Some metal wires have **plastic** on them. Wire cutters can strip off the plastic. The wire will not get cut.

Hand Saws

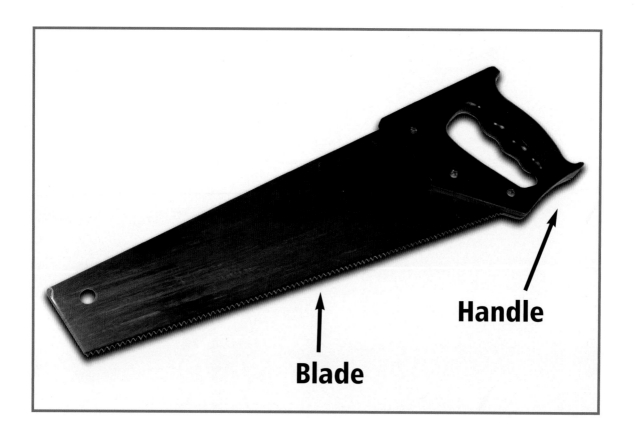

Handle

Blade

A hand saw has a **blade** and a **handle**. Carpenters use saws to cut wood.

Sharp teeth on the blade cut through wood.
Carpenters need strong muscles to move the saw
back and forth.

Electric Saws

Some saws use **electricity** to move. Electricity moves this saw around and around.

Electricity moves this saw up and down. It cuts wood into curved shapes.

Portable Gas Saws

This is a chain saw. A chain saw can quickly cut down a big tree. A motor turns a sharp chain to cut the wood.

This is a pole saw. It has a small saw on the end.
People use it to cut tall branches.

Axes and Wedges

An axe has a sharp blade on a long handle. People use axes to chop wood.

A wedge cuts wood, too. But you need a hammer to hit the wedge into the wood.

Jackhammers

This is a jackhammer. Workers use it to break up **concrete**. It is very loud!

This is a jackhammer, too. But it is much bigger. It is used for big jobs.

Be Safe With Tools

You should have an adult help you with any tools. You should wear gloves and goggles to protect yourself.

GLOSSARY

blade (BLAYD) — sharp part of a tool

concrete (kon KREET) — mixture of rocks and cement used for making sidewalks and roads

edge (EJ) — thin sharp side of a blade

electrician (i lek TRISH uhn) — person who works with electricity

electricity (i lek TRISS uh tee) — a type of energy

handle (HAN duhl) — the part of a tool that is held you hold

metal (MET uhl) — hard, shiny material used to make wires and blades

plastic (PLASS tik) — colorful material that can cover wires

tool (TOOL) — something that helps people do work

INDEX

FURTHER READING

Miller, Heather. *Construction Worker.* Heinemann: Chicago, 2002.
Redmond, Dianne. *Bob the Builder: Bob's Tools*.
    BBC Consumer Publishing: London, 2001.
Snyder, Inez. *Building Tools.* Children's Press: New York, 2002.

WEBSITES TO VISIT

www.thewoodcrafter.net/jr.html
www.bobthebuilder.com/usa/index.html
www.buildeazy.com/kidsdiy_diyprojects.html

ABOUT THE AUTHOR

Patty Whitehouse has been a teacher for 17 years. She is currently a Lead Science teacher in Chicago, where she lives with her husband and two teenage children. She enjoys reading, gardening, and writing about science for children.